**Living Love Forward**

Finding the Gifts in the Yuck

A Children's Leadership Series

Written by Kim Dawson
Illustrated by Paige Anocibar

Publisher: Tandem Services Press
PO Box 220, Yucaipa, CA 92399
www.tandemservicesink.com

Book Design by Paige Anocibar

ISBN 978-1-954986-28-2

Appreciation to

To my mom, who recently passed away and who was one of my biggest fans. This was the last book she edited for me before she passed...Finding the Gifts in the Yuck...Thanks, Mom.

Inland Leaders Charter School and all our teachers and staff for inspiring me to write this series.

All my students and their families who taught me to be a better teacher and person.

The 3rd, 4th, and 5th grade classes at Inland Leaders who gave me GREAT feedback and helped me make this story better!

Pelican Elementary in Oregon for letting us use their school as a model for Lexie's Huckleberry Elementary.

My family and friends who have never wavered in supporting and encouraging my mission to help others.

Paige, my illustrator, for putting up with my "creative" tangents.

Jennifer Crosswhite, my editor and friend, who has been my sounding board and always keeps me positive when I hit the many bumps in the road. (https://www.tandemservicesink.com)

All my readers who have supported me and helped me spread the message that kids can be leaders too.

Sending a ton of love and encouragement to all of you!
We got this!

From the author of the series Living Love Forward:

I wrote this children's leadership series to create an open conversation about the experiences our kids face every day. Being a teacher for over two decades, I have created connections with kids of all ages. I have observed and learned a lot through these interactions and have discovered key skill sets that I think are important for their growth. My purpose in writing these sentimental and caring stories is the hope that they instill life skills and resilience in our children. In turn, this empowers them to become successful, compassionate, and strong leaders. Join Lexie and our children as they navigate this journey of self-discovery.

Please note that this series can be used in conjunction with any Leadership Program focused on survival skills and effective habits for children.

This book specifically focuses on:

- **Loss**
- **Sadness**
- **Depression**
- **Upset**
- **Crying**
- **Anxiety**
- **Frustration**
- **Healing**
- **Coping Skills**
- **Hope**

Map of Harlow

Train Station

Church of Hope

Cemetery

Liberty Library

Lexie's House

Bus Stop

Jackson Sports Park

Riverside Park

Huckleberry Elementary

Annabelle's House

1st Street

2nd Street

2nd Street

4th Street

Main Street

Main Street

Main Street

Rise Road

Rise Road

Rise Road

Daisy Lane

Lavendar Lane

Lavendar Lane

Lotus Loop

Lotus Loop

Jasmine Avenue

Jasmine Avenue

Jasmine Avenue

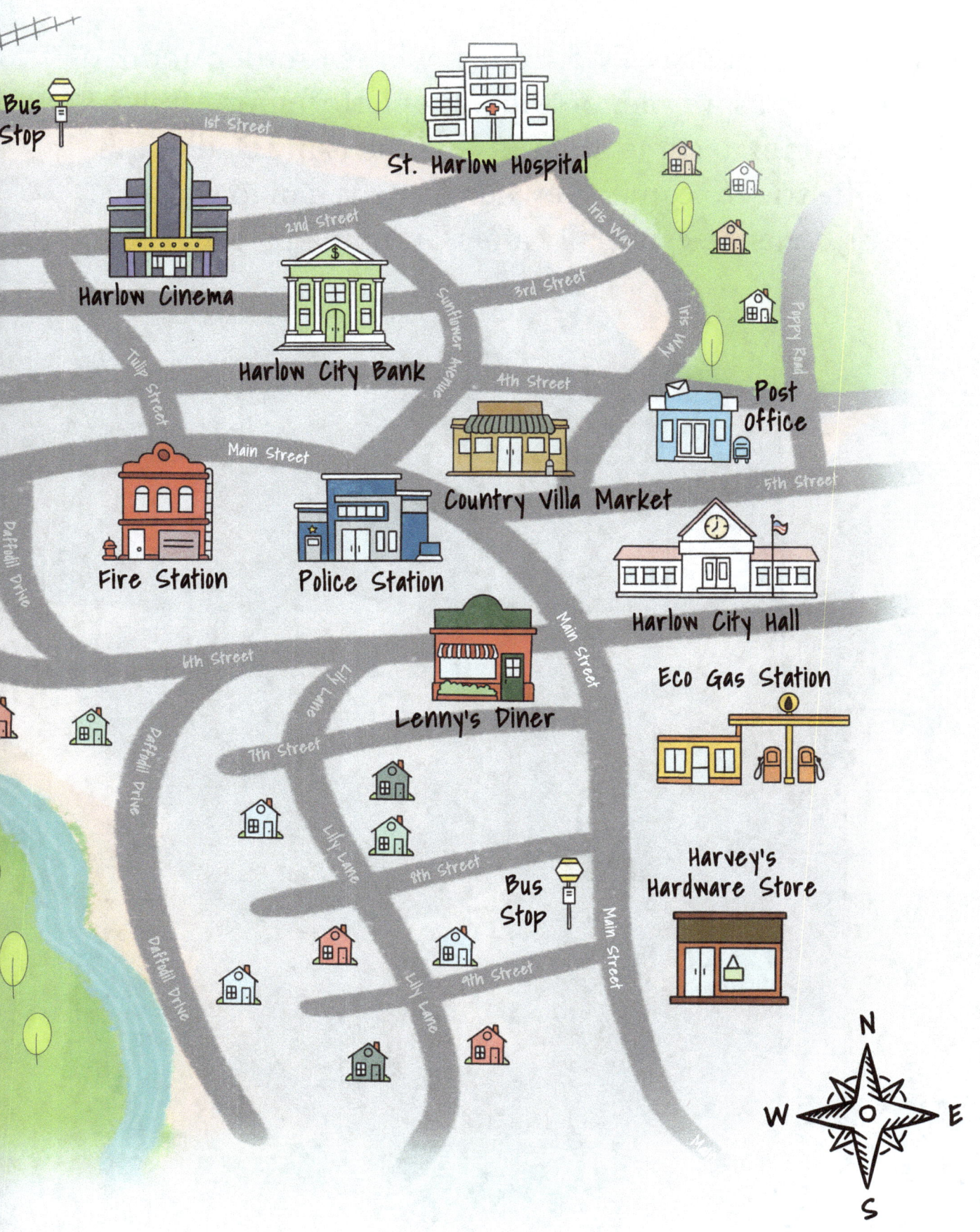

It is a dark, chilly day. Dad, Sam, my little brother, and I are shivering as we wait on the train platform for Aunt Claudia's train to come in. Aunt Claudia is my Dad's little sister. She tries to come out whenever she can to visit us. We miss her a lot, especially after Grandma passed.

Waiting there for her goes by slowly. We are bitter cold and the breeze keeps causing us to shake. Knowing she is coming to visit for the whole weekend, however, is just enough to keep us from complaining about the chilly weather. Finally, her train arrives and we watch for her to get off the train.

I see her first and start to shout, "Auntie! Aunt Claudia, over here!" I wave my hands over my head to try and catch her attention, but she doesn't see me. "Auntie!" I call out again and this time she hears me. She waves excitedly as she comes rushing over to us.

"Lexie, you have gotten so much taller since the last time I saw you!" she says as she sweeps me up into a big hug "Sam, come over here and give your Auntie a hug too!" Sam does it without hesitation and runs right up to hug her.

She is like a second mom to both of us and we have missed her tremendously. We have been waiting for weeks for her to finally get here. It is Dad's birthday this weekend and we are all going to celebrate it together. Clinging to each other, we excitedly make our way to the car.

On the ride home, we start to discuss what we are going to do for Dad's birthday. We come up with a lot of different ideas. As we pull into our driveway, Dad tells us, "I just want to do something low-key with my family."

Thinking about his request, we decide to stay home and make him dinner. Aunt Claudia promises she will help us make a birthday cake for him too.

With the plans set, we all settle in for the night and I snuggle on the couch with her.

She notices a photo album that Dad stores under the coffee table. Leaning over, she grabs it. I have looked at it a million times, but it is always fun to hear her share stories about the pictures in the album. She shuffles through the pages, stops, and points to a picture on the page. It is of Grandma. It seems like just yesterday that she passed and I miss going to her house every Friday for dinner. I still have the gray hat she gave me. I like to wear it to school on Fridays when I am missing her. I can tell Auntie is remembering some things too. She stares at the picture of Grandma for a long time.

She sighs as I ask her, "Do you miss her?"

She turns to me and whispers, "Every day." Then she smiles and hugs me. "It gets easier as time goes on, but it is still hard sometimes. I have found that if I can find the gifts in the yuck, it helps me feel better."

Not sure exactly what she means by that, I ask her, "Gifts in the yuck...what does that mean?"

I wait patiently while she collects her thoughts. Then she says, "Finding gifts in the yuck means that when you are sad because you are missing someone, you try and think of things about them that you are grateful for or memories that make you feel good instead. It is a kind of healing, where you turn your sad memories into happier ones. It is hard at first because you are missing them. Eventually, it gets easier, and thinking about them makes you smile more than cry. Those are the good days."

She continues by saying that it doesn't only have to be about losing someone though. "It can really be about anything. It's about turning a bad moment into a better moment" she shares.

I think about this for a bit. Then I say, "Kinda like when we were waiting for you at the train station and it was REALLY cold and dreary outside. Instead of complaining about how miserable we were, we talked about how good it would be to see you instead...like that?"

"That's a great example, Lexie. You got it," she encourages.

We lean back on the couch, her arm around me, and we both sit and think quietly in our heads. Eventually, I look at her and say **hesitantly**, "Kinda like mom...."

She looks at me for a second before she responds. Then she hugs me a bit tighter and says, "Yes, kinda like your mom. What gifts in the yuck can you think of with your mom?"

I don't remember her too much anymore. It is like her memory has started to fade. That makes me sad because I don't want to forget her.

I have mentioned this to Dad several times. Each time we pull out the photo album and find a picture of her, he helps me remember her. I love him for that.

I think about Aunt Claudia's question. What gifts in the yuck can I think of regarding Mom? I contemplate my answer to her question and say, "We both liked the color purple." I think some more, "I know she loves me wherever she is. Dad told me that too." I finish with, "I wouldn't have Sam, Dad, or even you if it wasn't for Mom."

Aunt Claudia holds me tightly and says, "There you go. You just found three gifts in the yuck. I know you wish your mom were here, Lexie. I wish she were too. She isn't, though, and there isn't anything you or I can do about that. It isn't fair and it makes us VERY sad and even mad sometimes. However, healing comes when we can find positive things to think about, instead of focusing on the sadness of missing them. It doesn't change anything, but it can help." I nod in understanding.

There you go. You just found three gifts in the yuck.

"So, Auntie, you are saying that whenever I miss her and start to feel sad, I just stop and think of something happy about her."

Whenever I miss her and start to feel sad, I just stop and think of something happy about her?

"That's the idea, kiddo. It isn't always easy and it will take some practice for sure. I have discovered, though, that with time you start thinking of the gifts more than the sadness or yuck without even trying. That is a clear sign that you are healing." She pauses and then continues by saying, "You know, Lexie, I still cry sometimes when I think about Grandma, but not as much as I used to. I still get upset sometimes when I think about your mom too," she shares.

That's the idea, kiddo.

Dad comes in then and lets us know it is time for bed. I grumble, but get up to hug him goodnight. I hug Auntie again and stand up to head off to bed. Dad glances at the photo album on the table as he and I walk to the hallway. He looks at his sister and she smiles weakly at him. I catch this, out of the corner of my eye, as I walk past. This is hard on all of us.

The next morning is bright and crisp. We are excited to get started on Dad's big day. First, we head to Country Villa Market to get everything we need for dinner and Dad's birthday cake.

Once we get home and everything is sorted, we get to work. Dad is relaxing in the living room watching a football game.

Time flies and before long, the kitchen is a mess, but the food smells amazing and delicious. Sam and I set the table and make a big Happy Birthday sign for Dad which we hang on the wall. It isn't the first time we have had a party in the kitchen, but it has been a while since we had one with Aunt Claudia here. Dad's birthday cake is the best part! It looks and smells so good. It is Dad's favorite, chocolate with strawberries inside. I can't wait for him to try it. We are almost set and then we hear his cell phone ring. Sometimes Dad gets called in for emergencies at the hospital he works at. He is a nurse in the Emergency Room at St. Harlow's Hospital. Our fingers are crossed that this isn't one of those calls. We hear him talking and then he comes into the kitchen. We know as soon as he comes in that something has happened.

"I have to go in. There was a big accident and they are shorthanded," he explains with a sigh. We are all disappointed.

"...but it is your birthday!" Sam shouts. "Can't they find someone else?"

Kneeling down to Sam, Dad says, "I wish they could, Buddy, but they need me. I am bummed too. I promise I will come back as soon as I can."

We are all feeling down as we walk Dad to his car.

Aunt Claudia waves us back into the house as he leaves, knowing the party is ruined. We sit on the couch to watch a movie and wait for Dad to come home. We decide to wait until Dad comes back to eat dinner. Auntie prepares some snacks for us to eat, so we don't get too hungry as we wait. When the movie ends, there is still no sign of Dad. Aunt Claudia gets a strange look on her face and springs up off the couch so quickly, it surprises us. She says, "I have an idea! If your dad can't be here, then why can't we bring the party to him? Come on, you guys. Let's go find some of those gifts in the yuck." We nod in agreement and grab what we need.

Let's go find some of those gifts in the yuck.

I grab the cake from the counter. Sam snatches some paper plates and plastic spoons from the drawer. Auntie swipes the car keys from the hook. We quickly put on our shoes and jackets, and race to Grandma's old car which is still parked in our driveway. Dad isn't ready to get rid of it yet. So, Aunt Claudia uses it when she comes to stay with us.

Aunt Claudia heads down the street and we are silent in anticipation. Soon we are pulling into St. Harlow's Hospital parking lot. She herds us through the Emergency Room doors and goes straight up to the help window. She asks for Dad and explains why we are here. The nurse on duty sees the birthday cake and our smiling faces and grins. She makes a call and we wait in the lobby for Dad.

Aunt Claudia whispers to us that when Dad comes out, we are going to sing Happy Birthday to him as loudly as we can. She says that if it is off-key...even better! We are ready!

Dad pops his head out and looks at us strangely. We immediately start to sing, "Happy birthday to you. Happy birthday to you..." It is loud and super off-key, but everyone around us is laughing and smiling. Dad mostly. He comes over to hug us after we get done singing. He says, "Well, it wasn't the birthday that we planned, but what a way to celebrate. Oh, and by the way, you guys can't sing AT ALL!" he teases us. In the lobby, we eat a piece of cake together and share the rest with the staff who are working tonight.

Dad has to leave and Aunt Claudia ushers us out to the car. When we get in, I say to her, "Auntie, I think this is a great example of finding gifts in the yuck! We were sad because Dad had to go to work and we couldn't have his birthday party. So, instead of staying sad, we brought the party to him and celebrated at the hospital. Don't you think this a good example?"

She smiles and responds, "Lexie, this is a perfect example! Always look for those gifts in the yuck, Sweetheart. It really does help."

I lean back in my seat and smile knowing we just saved Dad's birthday.

Always look for those gifts in the yuck, sweetheart.

Author's Advice

- Healing comes from switching the bad memories with good ones

- Life is a bunch of opportunities to look in a new direction

- Don't be afraid to struggle, because with struggle comes strength

- If you are struggling, try doing something nice for someone else and notice how that feels

- Find your happy place again

Can you think of a time when you struggled with something that upset you? Can you find the "gifts in the yuck" when you think about it? Talk to someone about what you discover.

Glossary

contemplate

Definition: to look at or think about carefully for a long time

Part of Speech:

This word is a (noun, adjective, verb, adverb).

Evidence of how the word is used in the story.

Lexie contemplates (thinks carefully about) Aunt Claudia's question about her mom.

crisp

Definition: clear and cool; cold; brisk.

Part of Speech:

This word is a (noun, adjective, verb, adverb).

Evidence of how the word is used in the story.

The morning of Dad's birthday is bright and crisp (clear and cool).

Glossary

dreary

Definition: gloomy; bleak

Part of Speech:

This word is a (noun, adjective, verb, adverb).

Evidence of how the word is used in the story.

It was a cold and dreary (gloomy) day as they were waiting for Aunt Claudia's train to arrive.

hesitantly

Definition: not feeling sure; in doubt

Part of Speech:

This word is a (noun, adjective, verb, adverb).

Evidence of how the word is used in the story.

When Lexie and Aunt Claudia talk about Lexie's mom, she does it hesitantly (with doubt).

Glossary

low-key

Definition: laid-back; mild; quiet; relaxed

Part of Speech:

This word is a (noun, adjective, verb, adverb).

Evidence of how the word is used in the story.

Dad wants a low-key birthday party where he is just relaxing with his family.

off-key

Definition: not in tune: not on the right musical note or pitch; flat or sharp

Part of Speech:

This word is a (noun, adjective, verb, adverb).

Evidence of how the word is used in the story.

Lexie, Sam, and Aunt Claudia sing the birthday song to Dad off-key (not in tune).

Glossary

shorthanded

Definition: not having enough workers or helpers.

Part of Speech:

This word is a (noun, adjective, verb, adverb).

Evidence of how the word is used in the story.

The hospital staff is shorthanded (doesn't have enough workers), so Dad has to go to work on his birthday.

tremendously

Definition: immensely; in a big way; very large degree; huge amount;

Part of Speech:

This word is a (noun, adjective, verb, adverb).

Evidence of how the word is used in the story.

Sam and Lexie miss Aunt Claudia tremendously (in a big way).

Glossary

ushers

Definition: to lead, escort, or show

Part of Speech:

This word is a (noun, adjective, verb, adverb).

Evidence of how the word is used in the story.

Aunt Claudia ushers (leads) Lexie and Sam into the house after Dad leaves to go to the hospital on his birthday.

yuck

Definition: Something that isn't likable; something gross and unpleasant

Part of Speech:

This word is a (noun, adjective, verb, adverb).

Evidence of how the word is used in the story.

Aunt Claudia tells Lexie that part of healing from something sad or bad is to find the gifts in the yuck (something not likable and unpleasant)

About the Author: Kim Dawson

I am a single mom of two wonderful kids. I have been teaching for a number of decades and love spending time with my students. I have been writing since I was a child. It has always been a way for me to express myself when I am struggling. I strongly believe that we do not give our kids the credit they deserve. They have a lot to teach us if we just listen.

About the Illustrator: Paige Anocibar

Art is my passion. Every day I am thankful to have a career that empowers me to express myself through creativity. Drawing has been a part of my life since I was a small child. Coloring and painting were my favorite part of going to school. Back then, just like now, I was eager for the next art project. I knew that expressing myself through art is all I have ever wanted to do with my life, and illustrating this book has helped me achieve a part of that dream.

If you enjoyed this story, see other books in this Children's Leadership series, Living Love Forward.

2023 Books

2024 Books

2025 Books

www.ingramcontent.com/pod-product-compliance
Lightning Source LLC
Chambersburg PA
CBHW081011120626
46546CB00010B/3106